NINTENDO

ABDO
Publishing Company

TECHNOLOGY
PIONEERS

NINTENDO

THE COMPANY AND ITS FOUNDERS

by Mary Firestone

Content Consultant
Jason Begy
Research Associate
Singapore-MIT GAMBIT Game Lab

CREDITS

Published by ABDO Publishing Company, 8000 West 78th Street, Edina, Minnesota 55439. Copyright © 2011 by Abdo Consulting Group, Inc. International copyrights reserved in all countries. No part of this book may be reproduced in any form without written permission from the publisher. The Essential Library™ is a trademark and logo of ABDO Publishing Company.

Printed in the United States of America,
North Mankato, Minnesota
112010
012011

 THIS BOOK CONTAINS AT LEAST 10% RECYCLED MATERIALS.

Editor: Mari Kesselring
Copy Editor: Chelsey Whitcomb
Interior Design and Production: Kazuko Collins
Cover Design: Emily Love

Library of Congress Cataloging-in-Publication Data
Firestone, Mary.
  Nintendo : the company and its founders / by Mary Firestone.
    p. cm. -- (Technology pioneers)
  Includes bibliographical references and index.
  ISBN 978-1-61714-809-5
  1. Nintendo of America Inc. 2. Nintendo Kabushiki Kaisha.
  3. Electronic games industry--United States. 4. Electronic games industry--Japan. I. Title.
  HD9993.E454N573 2011
  338.7'6179480973--dc22
                                       2010044664

TABLE OF CONTENTS

People stood in line at a Game Stop in Los Angeles, California, for the West Coast release of the Nintendo Wii.

WELCOMING THE WII

Just before midnight on November 17, 2006, a long line had formed outside the Toys R Us store in Manhattan's Times Square. In the last few hours, the crowd had gotten noisy. Some of the people had been waiting in line for more than a week. Blankets, pillows, and chairs lined the sidewalk. But the long wait and New York's cold November air did little to chill the excitement of the crowd.

Why were so many people willing to wait outside for days in the November cold? A huge, brightly lit "Wii" sign near the store entrance was the answer. It was the US launch party for the new Nintendo game console— the Wii.

A loud, second-by-second countdown soon exploded from the crowd. At exactly midnight, the Toys R Us doors flew open. The obsessed gamers would soon be rewarded for their long wait as they became the first people to own a Nintendo Wii.

WII MORE THAN ANYTHING

A market research firm called Smarty Pants focuses on brands marketed to kids. In a 2009 study they called "Young Love," the company surveyed 4,700 kids between the ages of 6 and 12. The kids were asked how much they loved more than 200 major brands. Nintendo came out on top, with Nintendo Wii first and Nintendo DS second. These two Nintendo products came out ahead of time-tested kid favorites such as McDonald's, Nickelodeon, macaroni and cheese, and Disney. Mario came in at number 50, the GameCube at 76, and Nintendogs at 96.

NEW FEATURES

Nintendo had released many video game systems before the Wii, and they had been successful.

WII FLAWS

Not everyone thinks the Wii is so great. The consumer reporting site wiisucks.com provides descriptions of user disappointments. Some complaints include the cost of AA batteries to run the Wii remote and general annoyance with the motion-sensing controllers, which can fly out of a user's hand and hit the television if the wrist strap is not used.

In 1990, a study showed that Nintendo's Mario was more familiar to US kids than Disney's Mickey Mouse. Still, the Wii was something entirely new for Nintendo. Its unique feature was its ability to detect human motion in three dimensions. No other system on the market could do that. Moving the slim, wireless remote control up, down, or back and forth would cause a proportional movement on-screen, without pushing any buttons. Instead of pushing a button, a swing of the player's wrist caused a ball to fly across the digital golf course.

Another advantage of the Wii was its low cost compared to other systems at the time. It also appealed to young and old alike, with a variety of games that made it easy to play as a family or to get some exercise while remaining indoors.

THE MOM RULE

While developing the new generation console, Nintendo had considered many of its different functions. To compete with other video game giants such as Microsoft and Sony, Nintendo would have to produce something with a lot of power. But power did not win out in the final phase. Nintendo's game designer, Shigeru Miyamoto, explained that the concept ended up focusing on a new form of player interaction instead. "The consensus was that power isn't everything for a console. Too many powerful consoles can't coexist. It's like having only ferocious dinosaurs. They might fight and hasten their own extinction."[1]

Miyamoto also knew that more power would require including a fan in the design, which would increase

WHAT IS IN A NAME?

The gaming world was expecting Nintendo to follow through with its original prerelease name, Revolution, a much bolder title, when they changed the name to Wii. Many people wondered why Nintendo chose such an unusual name for the new system.

"It doesn't make any sense," one blogger complained.[2] "Worst console name ever," Chris Remo, editor of shacknews.com, said of Wii.[3] Gaming forums on the Internet exploded with jokes. Was it pronounced *why* or *wee*? Did they want players to think of the kind of *wheeee* a kid makes jumping off a swing? Or worse, *wee wee*?

Nintendo of America (NOA) president, Reggie Fils-Aime, explained the decision to change the name to Wii. "Revolution as a name is not ideal," he said. "It's long, and in some cultures, it's hard to pronounce. So we wanted something that was short, to the point, easy to pronounce, and distinctive."[4] Nintendo expected a negative reaction, so they announced the name change eight months before the launch. By the time the lines were forming in Times Square on the launch date, all the upset and the jokes about the silly name were old news.

Miyamoto worked for Nintendo for several decades
before helping to create and promote the Wii.

the system's noise. "Moms would rise up against it.
Plus, it would take too long to boot up, like a PC,
which isn't an ideal toy," he said in a 2006 interview
with *Businessweek*.[5] In the end, the Wii did have a
fan, but it was quieter than competing systems' fans.
Still, getting parents' approval for the Wii remained
Miyamoto's critical goal. He explained,

> *We talked about what specs and features a console
> should have. But we knew we would get nowhere
> if we didn't get moms' approval. So we thought
> about what might convince moms to buy this for
> their kids. When that happened, we talked about*

basic concepts and goals, not about the technical specifications of the console. This was the Wii's first major step.[6]

NINTENDO AND THE WORLD

Nintendo's journey to creating the Wii had been a long road for an old company. During its more than 100-year existence, Nintendo revolutionized the entertainment industry by producing innovative games that employed wit and humor. Until Nintendo came along, most games on the market focused on violent forms of entertainment, such as shooting gaming. Although Nintendo also played a big part in producing violent games, it made an effort to create many games and characters appropriate for younger audiences. When the Super Mario Brothers game was introduced in 1985, the industry saw an unusual lead

WII REMOTES

The Nintendo designers did their best to make the Wii controller as visually appealing as possible. They were aware that people who did not play video games were not inclined to pick up a game controller, except to put it away where it would not be seen. The designers compared television remotes to game controllers and considered how television remotes were allowed to remain out in the open, lying on couches, coffee tables, or even the floor. Sometimes the problem people had with video game controllers were the long wires from the controller to the console, strewn across the floor. To make the controller for the Wii more attractive and user-friendly, designer Satoru Iwata decided to make it slim and wireless, just like a television remote. The result was the sleek, rectangular Wii remote.

character: a little plumber who used his skills to fight and outwit his enemies. As the Mario sequels were released, the company grew, and by the early 1990s, it was netting more profits than US film studios. Nintendo had become a home entertainment giant.

The success of Nintendo had a worldwide impact, with companies developing new consoles and games to compete with this industry leader. Many experts in the computer industry believe that Nintendo was successful because it retained control over both the hardware (the game systems) and the software (the games). However, Nintendo began as a small, family company long before the days of high-tech entertainment. +

Nintendo fans all over the world could not wait to purchase the Wii.

Hanafuda are smaller and thicker than Western playing cards.

PLAYING CARDS

Every invention starts as an idea for improvement. Someone begins to sketch or tinker with an existing product and soon a new product comes into being. These new products often lead to advances in technology. Companies are formed and factories are built for making a new product. It is a long process, but eventually the product is ready to be sold. How successful the product is depends on its quality, how it is advertised, and whether there is consumer demand for it.

In Nintendo's case, this process actually happened twice. In a way, Nintendo has been two different companies: first, a small but growing playing card business, and second, a high-tech home entertainment giant.

MAKING PLAYING CARDS

It all began in 1889 when Fusajiro Yamauchi, a craftsman in the Japanese city of Kyoto, created his own brand of handmade playing cards known as *hanafuda*. Smaller than regular playing cards, they had pictures of cherry blossoms, deer, birds, and other nature

KYOTO

Kyoto is located in the center of Japan, and for most of its history, it was the country's capitol. The history of the city can be traced as far back as the sixth century. Kyoto is known as a spiritual center and for its large number of ancient Buddhist temples. The best-known temple in Kyoto is a Zen temple called Kinkaku-ji, or "the Golden Pavilion." It is covered with gold leaf.

HANAFUDA

Hanafuda playing cards were the sole source of Nintendo's business for nearly 100 years, and the company still makes hanafuda today. Hanafuda come in decks consisting of 12 different suits of four cards each, for a total of 48 cards per deck. The suits are named after the month in which a particular flower blooms, and pictures of the flowers are on each card. Hanafuda cards are much thicker and smaller than Western playing cards.

In the early days, making the cards began with pounding the bark from a mulberry tree into a paste. The paste was mixed with clay and shaped into layers. The layers were pushed together to create the hard back of the card. When dry and cut, the cards were painted with color inks. Then, they were packaged and sold. *Hanafuda* means "flower cards."

images painted on them. These symbolic images stood for different things, such as good fortune or long life. Hanafuda were used for playing matching games and more complicated card games.

When Yamauchi chose the company name, Nintendo Koppai, he used kanji characters. These are a type of Chinese lettering that is also used in Japanese writing. Each kanji character in *nin-ten-do koppai* has meaning. The company name means, "Leave luck to heaven."

Yamauchi's cards must have been very well made, because they became the most popular cards in Kyoto. Yamauchi's business was blossoming, and when the Japanese mafia, or yakuza, began using hanafuda in gambling casinos, his business boomed. Gamblers used a lot of cards because they started each game with a brand-new deck.

With the demand for hanafuda increasing, Yamauchi

hired and trained new employees, who then produced the cards in much greater numbers. In 1907, he expanded the company again to produce larger, American-style playing cards. Nintendo became the first company in Japan to produce Western-style playing cards. Around this time, Yamauchi also struck a profitable deal with a national tobacco operation, which made it possible for him to sell his cards in tobacco shops all over Japan.

A FAMILY BUSINESS

When Yamauchi was ready to retire, he wanted to pass the

HISTORY OF JAPANESE PLAYING CARDS

Centuries ago, Japanese nobility used playing cards for entertainment, but when Spanish explorers arrived in 1549, they brought Portuguese playing cards with them, called *Hombre*. They shared the cards and taught new card games to the Japanese, including gambling games, which became very popular. In 1633, Japan closed itself off from the Western world, and all forms of gambling with cards were banned—though playing cards without gambling was still allowed. People created new types of cards for this more innocent kind of playing, but eventually the cards would be used for gambling, too. Once a type of cards became popular and identified by the government as a tool for gambling, new cards were privately developed to conceal the practice.

The Japanese government eventually relaxed the laws slightly, resulting in the creation of hanafuda, which were legal. However, card games became less popular, and eventually, the public lost interest. The playing card business was revived when Fusajiro Yamauchi founded Nintendo Koppai in 1889, and the Japanese mafia began using large numbers of his cards in its casinos.

Nintendo began in the city of Kyoto in Japan.

company along to a member of his family. His only problem was that he had two daughters and no sons. In those days in Japan, businesses could not be passed along to daughters. The only way to keep the business in the family would be for one of Yamauchi's daughters to marry a man capable of running the business.

Yamauchi's daughter Tei eventually married a man named Sekiryo Kaneda. On the day they were married, he took her family name. This was the custom when a man took over his wife's family business. Her husband's name became Sekiryo Yamauchi, and he took over as the president of Nintendo in 1929.

The company's playing card business prospered under Sekiryo. He built new offices and a distribution branch called Marufuku, which carried many new varieties of modern playing cards. He opened a factory with an assembly line and created levels of managers who competed continuously, trying to outperform each other.

Tei and Sekiryo's marriage also did not produce sons. Their daughter, Kimi, married Shikanojo Inaba, a young man from a family of respected craftspeople. When he married Kimi, his last name also became Yamauchi, but he did not take ownership of Nintendo. Then, in 1927 when Kimi and Shikanojo's son, Hiroshi, was born, he became the first male heir born into the Nintendo family business.

NINTENDO'S HEIR

Like most parents, Kimi and Shikanojo dreamed of a successful future for their baby son, Hiroshi. Little did they realize that most of the company's growth

MATERNAL STRENGTH

Hiroshi's grandmother, Tei Yamauchi, was a strong woman. When World War II broke out in 1939, the rest of Tei's family went underground as the sirens rang all night in Kyoto. But Tei refused to let her life be disrupted, going about her business as if nothing at all was unusual. She also protected Hiroshi from going to war by forcing him to stay in school until the war ended in 1945.

would occur under Hiroshi's strong leadership, eventually making him one of the richest men in the world. However, there would be bumps along the road to his success.

When Hiroshi was only five years old, Shikanojo ran away from home, abandoning his young wife and son. Kimi was unable to raise Hiroshi on her own, and she turned him over to her parents, the strict Tei and Sekiryo. However, their conservative approach to child rearing brought out the rebel in young Hiroshi. As he grew into his teenage years, he became the opposite of the modest Japanese gentleman he was raised to be by his grandparents. He developed a brash lifestyle that made a spectacle of his wealth. He carried himself publicly with an arrogant, devil-may-care attitude.

A NEW ERA

Despite his rebellious, spoiled ways, Hiroshi
appeared to value succeeding on his own. In 1945,
he enrolled in law school at Waseda University in
Tokyo. There were no plans in play at the time for
running his family's company.

When Sekiryo suffered a stroke and was near
death, he contacted Hiroshi, his only grandson. He
wanted to pass the business on to him, his only male
heir. Hiroshi agreed, but only if his grandfather
fired a family member, an older cousin who was still
working at Nintendo. Hiroshi did not want anyone
to question who was in charge of the new company,
and firing the only other blood relative would
secure his position as the man in charge. Employees
had heard rumors that their new leader would fire
every manager, and the rumors were true. Hiroshi
had his cousin fired, and then he proceeded to fire
every manager with a link to the conservative style
of the previous leadership. Hiroshi wanted to run
the company his own way. He did not want to fight
about the old, conservative way of doing things.

Hiroshi, only 21 years old, became president
of Nintendo in 1949, running the company with
strict, imperial control. He made all decisions. His

concerns about employees from his grandfather's era continued, however. The remaining employees did not view his presence as a positive change for the company. +

Hiroshi Yamauchi, 1997

Yamauchi struck a deal with the Walt Disney Company to allow Nintendo to put Disney characters, such as Minnie and Mickey Mouse, on playing cards.

HIROSHI YAMAUCHI RULES

As the company's new president, Hiroshi Yamauchi did more than change the faces at Nintendo. He opened new corporate offices and gave the company a new name, Nintendo Karuta. After trying out a few experimental ventures in other types of businesses, Yamauchi finally settled on the entertainment industry as Nintendo's main focus. Under his leadership, Nintendo would be the first to introduce plastic playing cards in Japan. He also acquired legal permission from the Walt Disney Company to use Disney characters on the plastic cards. In 1963, the company name was changed again to Nintendo Company Ltd (NCL).

TOY MAKERS

For all of his harshness and high expectations, Yamauchi had unusual faith in creative minds. An electronics specialist and inventor named Gunpei Yokoi came to Nintendo in 1965, looking for a job. Yokoi was hired as a janitor, but also as a technician to maintain the machines on the assembly line.

One day, in approximately 1966, Yamauchi asked Yokoi to come to his office. He asked Yokoi to make something that could be sold around the holiday season. When Yokoi asked what he should

DEALING WITH COMPETITION

Yamauchi's business agreement with the Walt Disney Company proved to be a good one. Disney cartoon characters were world famous, and their images made the Nintendo cards much more appealing to the youth market. Yamauchi also improved the look of the cards with a clear plastic coating, advertised them on television, and sold them in toy stores. Yamauchi's company's card sales were record breaking in 1959, at 600,000 packs of cards sold that year.

The inventors at Nintendo worked hard to impress Yamauchi, *left*.

make, Yamauchi's only response was, "Something great."[1]

Yokoi went on to develop a retractable hand toy called Ultra Hand, which was released in 1966. The "hand" could be extended to grasp things when two levers on each side were pressed, similar to a scissors. Pressing the levers exposed a lattice of plastic, which could fold up or extend. The toy was extremely popular in Japan. The company eventually sold 1.2 million Ultra Hands.

Around this time, Yamauchi put Yokoi in charge of 30 engineers at Nintendo, a group called Research and Development Team 1 (R & D 1). R & D 1 would go down in history for producing some of the best toys and games in Nintendo's repertoire. But even though Yamauchi appreciated the engineers' skills and inventions, he drove his young product development team like a taskmaster. He focused on their skills as individuals, never actually promoting a team approach. This created a sense of competition and the desire to please the driven Yamauchi. This desire to please the company's owner was a sentiment felt throughout the engineering staff and among other employees. One claimed that they all "lived for his praise."[2]

IMPRESSING YAMAUCHI

Trying to impress Yamauchi, Yokoi moved on to other inventions based on the Ultra theme. Yokoi invented the Ultra Machine, which pitched baseballs that were soft so the toy could be used indoors with a bat. Next, Yokoi invented the Ultra Scope. It was similar to a regular periscope, but it had a unique refocusing function, which allowed kids to see around corners.

Yamauchi's instinct told him the Ultra toys would be a success. These instincts came into play regularly. He gave Yokoi suggestions, and Yokoi would go off to tinker and come up with something he thought would please Yamauchi. Yokoi claims that Yamauchi never asked what others thought of his choices of products to develop; if Yamauchi liked it, it was developed and marketed.

Yokoi had earned Yamauchi's faith. Soon, he started tinkering with electronics, and eventually he came up with a device called the Love Tester. It was meant to reveal how much two people loved each other. The Love Tester had two handles, and each

YAMAUCHI'S EXPERIMENTS

Before Yamauchi settled on entertainment and games for Nintendo, he changed the company name from Nintendo Karuta, which meant "Nintendo Playing Cards," to Nintendo Company Ltd. He also took the company public, which gave him the financial resources he needed to expand into different product types.

One of these products was a type of instant rice, which was sold in individual portions. The product was a failure. Yamauchi also started a taxi business, which he named Daiya. This was a successful venture, but he sold it when struggles with the driver labor unions made the business too expensive to run. Another business idea of Yamauchi's was something called a "love hotel." Most hotels rented rooms by the night, but love hotels rented rooms by the hour. Yamauchi was a married man, but he was known for his many infidelities. It is said that he was one of the love hotels' best customers. This business also came to an end, as Yamauchi decided that the company should continue its historic focus on entertainment and games.

person would take a handle in one hand, and then hold their partner's other hand to complete the circuit. The amount of current passing between the two people was revealed on a meter, and this was meant to show the amount of love between them. The test was not accurate, but it was a lot of fun at parties. It was a huge success in Japan where public handholding was considered risqué.

MEET MASAYUKI UEMURA

A young engineer named Masayuki Uemura walked into Nintendo's office one day in the early 1970s to sell solar cell products produced by the company Sharp. Solar cells are devices that convert light into electricity. Uemura and Yokoi discussed how the cells might be used in toys. This was a pivotal moment in Uemura's life. Before long, he was working for Nintendo.

Yokoi and Uemura began working together to develop solar cell applications for toys. They found that solar cells did away with

SOLAR CELLS

Solar cells convert light into electricity through a process known as photovoltaic effect, which was discovered in 1839 by a French physicist named Edmund Becquerel. The light source is most often the sun but indoor lighting of different kinds may also work. Light has units of energy called photons, which are absorbed by the solar cell. When light hits the cell, photon energy displaces the cell's electrons. This activity eventually generates an electric current.

MASAYUKI UEMURA

Masayuki Uemura was born in Nara, Japan, in 1943. He moved with his family to Kyoto to escape the bombing during World War II. His family was poor, and the young Uemura did not have toys. He used his imagination to create toys of his own. He even made radio-controlled airplanes from stray pieces of junk he had found. He was eventually trained as an electronics technician, and then got a good job at Sharp selling electronic parts. In 1972, he went on to lead Research and Development Team 2 (R & D 2) at Nintendo.

the need for wires and expensive batteries and had the advantage of being lightweight as well. Nintendo tried the technology out on a shooting game, which evolved to the Nintendo Beam Gun. It was a version of popular shooting games from arcades, where players pointed a toy gun at a screen to hit objects on it, but it was made for home televisions. This successful product sold more than 1 million units.

Uemura later remarked how Nintendo was unique among entertainment companies in Japan. He said Nintendo had a knack for coming up with completely original ideas, like the Beam Gun, while other companies were busy trying to adapt their products to US versions.

SOLAR CELLS AND SHOOTING GAMES

Thinking of ways to improve and expand on ideas, Yokoi discovered that the solar cell technology used in the Beam Gun could be used for other entertainment purposes. First, he tried skeet shooting. Skeet is a shooting game where clay disks called pigeons are ejected from a machine. Shooters do their best to hit the disks. Yokoi brought the skeet idea to Yamauchi, who thought up ways in which it could be applied for consumer use.

Bowling had once been a popular fad in Japan, but interest in the game was waning. Yamauchi decided to turn vacant bowling alleys into skeet shooting galleries. Images of clay pigeons would appear at the end of the lanes instead of bowling pins, and shooters would practice their aim with toy guns instead of bowling balls. Solar cells with built-in detection systems could keep track of how many hits were made while keeping score electronically. The system technology turned out to be a challenge, since the light beam that the gun emitted when it was fired had to match the sound effect of a gun firing. But, the designers eventually solved the problem.

When the design was perfected in 1973, Nintendo set up its first Laser Clay Range in Kyoto. However, on the first demonstration for the public, the game malfunctioned. Nintendo engineer Genyo Takeda quickly jumped behind the targets. Unseen

GENYO TAKEDA

Genyo Takeda was born in 1949 in Osaka, Japan. He graduated in 1970 with an engineering degree from the Shizuoka Government University. He came to Nintendo by answering a newspaper advertisement the company had placed for a toy designer.

Takeda eventually led one of Nintendo's famous Research and Development teams, R & D 3. Takeda worked with the mechanical aspects of creating games. He and his R & D team created the first mechanics for what would become Famicom, Japan's popular video game console, but he also tinkered with game development. As of 2010, Takeda still worked at Nintendo, serving as Research and Development general manager.

by spectators, he managed to make the game work manually. It was an illusion that paid off very well, because the Laser Clay Ranges were a success from the first day, eventually becoming entertainment hot spots in Kyoto. However, Nintendo would soon move on to even bigger things. +

Shooting games became popular in Japan following
the launch of the Laser Clay Range in 1973.

From left, Federico Faggin, Marcian Edward Hoff Jr., and Stanley Mazor, the coinventors of the Intel microprocessor

NEW TECHNOLOGY

Yamauchi and his staff continued to hire designers to work on more electronic toys and games. An important determinant of a game's success, they discovered, was how much they enjoyed creating and playing it themselves. Their approach to game design was paying off, and the company needed to expand again to accommodate the public's demand for more products.

Meanwhile, the combination of creative energy at Nintendo and the technological explosion happening globally at the time would soon become Nintendo's stepping-stone to the top of the home entertainment industry. Yamauchi was the first to recognize this important component of creative success in his developers.

A SHIFT IN FORTUNES

When the Japanese economy suffered through an oil shortage in the early 1970s, consumers had less money to spend on entertainment. The once popular and buzzing shooting galleries were now completely empty. Nintendo had not seen this disaster coming, and it looked as if the company might collapse altogether.

However, there was hope on the horizon. During the 1970s, the electronics industry was

NO ONE IS TOO OLD

Miyamoto says that adults respond to his games because they are "a trigger to again become primitive, primal, as a way of thinking and remembering. An adult is a child who has more ethics and morals. That's all. When I am a child, creating, I am not creating a game. I am in the game. The game is not for children, it is for me. It is for the adult that still has a character of a child."[1]

exploding. One of the most important developments was microelectronics, which reduced massive and complicated computer wiring to small integrated circuits. This made computer processing a lot cheaper, since integrated circuits were tiny and could also be mass-produced. The silicon semiconductors used in them were also inexpensive, since silicon is abundant in nature.

Intel, a manufacturer of semiconductors, developed the first microprocessor in 1971. A microprocessor is a key component to a computer. Reducing the computer's main processing unit to the size of a chip (about the size of your thumbnail) made technology more affordable in a variety of applications, including video games. Yamauchi was interested in these developments and how they might help him expand his company.

In 1975, Yamauchi attended a social gathering with another industry leader. At the gathering, he learned how the newest technologies used in other industries, such as consumer and office products, were becoming cheaper every year. He investigated the matter and found that Atari and Magnavox were already using these technologies in games that played on home televisions. Yamauchi acquired a license to distribute the Magnavox television games in Japan,

In the late 1970s, new technologies in Japan led
to more electronic products.

but at the same time, he had ambitions for unique
Nintendo products that made use of the newer
technologies.

COLOR TV GAMES

In 1977, Nintendo formed a partnership with the
Mitsubishi Electronics company to create its own
television game system. They released the Color TV

Game 6 in 1977, Nintendo's first ever video game console. It was a basic "pong" game, where a short beam of light was bounced back and forth across the television screen. Game 6 was unique because the games were in bright colors; most pong games at the time were in black and white. Two dials on each side provided game control, and toggle switches allowed players to control difficulty. Game 6 had six variations of pong games. Nintendo sold at least 1 million Color TV Game 6 systems. The game was a hit.

Game 6 was soon followed by the Color TV Game 15 that same year. These television games were followed by more complicated racing games. With the success of these new products, Nintendo had moved beyond

COLOR TV GAME 6 SPECS

Color TV Game 6 was the first home video game system released by Nintendo, and it had many features that appealed to its consumers. It included six classic games based on the "pong" template. All games could be played with either one or two players. These games were all included in the video game system. They did not need to be purchased separately like the later cartridge games.

Color TV Game 6 was very popular in Japan. However, in comparison to today's video game systems, Color TV Game 6 was cumbersome. Unlike most video game systems today, the Color TV Game 6 did not have a separate controller. Instead, players worked dials on the console itself to move their paddles on the screen. Players would have to sit very close together, both using dials on the same console. Today's video game controllers make playing games more comfortable.

playing cards and Beam Guns. The company had emerged as a contender in Japan's world of consumer electronics.

YAMAUCHI'S REVOLUTION

Nintendo was doing good business with its Beam Guns and TV Games, but Yamauchi was not satisfied simply with financial success in the brand-new era of electronic gaming. He wanted something that would revolutionize the industry. He continuously urged his engineers to keep up the hard work of creating something completely different. "Throw away all your old ideas in order to come up with something new," he said. "We must look in different directions."[2]

Yokoi later noted that one key to Nintendo's success was its ability to take advantage of established technologies, such as the miniaturized circuits for pocket calculators. Following Yamauchi's wishes, Yokoi went to work creating something "entirely new" but with existing and older technologies that could be mass-produced inexpensively.[3]

He achieved his and Yamauchi's goal in 1980 with a product they called the Game and Watch, which was no bigger than a pocket calculator. It

YOKOI'S LEGENDARY INSPIRATION

There is a legend in the gaming world about how the Nintendo Game and Watch came about. The legend says that while traveling on the train from Kyoto one day, Yokoi noticed a bored businessman entertaining himself with the buttons and lights on his handheld calculator. This sparked an idea. Yokoi soon developed a handheld version of video game systems. It began with the Game and Watch in 1980, which evolved into the Game Boy in 1989.

allowed players to enjoy killing a little time without losing track of it entirely.

At first, the Game and Watch handheld system was extremely simple. It had one button for the clock display, and two buttons for Game A and Game B. Game A was easier than Game B. This quickly evolved into two screens of equal size, and a more interesting variety of games and skill levels. The product caught on quickly, and Nintendo was ready to expand again with this new success. +

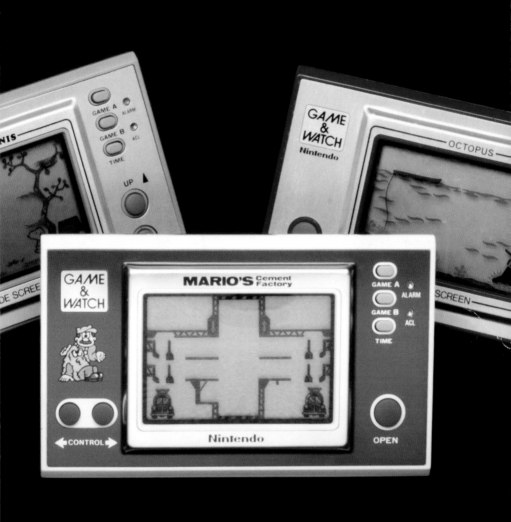

Nintendo produced several different versions of the Game and Watch.

Mino studied civil engineering at the Massachusetts
Institute of Technology.

NINTENDO
BRANCHES OUT

When Yamauchi's daughter, Yoko, wanted to marry the young Minoru (Mino) Arakawa in the early 1970s, Yamauchi was not pleased that Yoko had chosen Mino as her husband. Even though Mino was intelligent, treated Yoko well, and came from an aristocratic Kyoto family who had an established textile business called Arakawa Textiles, Yamauchi did not like him. He felt that anyone from an aristocratic family was arrogant. Yamauchi's wife had to convince him to give Mino permission to marry Yoko, as was the custom of the time.

MINORU ARAKAWA

Little did Yamauchi know, his son-in-law had an excellent background in business. Arakawa Textiles had a fine reputation for putting quality first and was well respected by other members of the business community. When the Arakawa family patriarch, Waichiro Arakawa, had retired some time earlier, his eldest son had taken over the family business, in accordance with Japanese tradition. Mino was the second son, so he was free to choose his career. After graduating from college in Kyoto, he headed to the United States. For graduate school, he attended the prestigious Massachusetts Institute of Technology (MIT), where he studied civil engineering. He toured the country in a Volkswagen bus on his vacations. He was fascinated with US culture and its emphasis on the individual. It was unlike the conformity that was generally expected of the Japanese. Mino eventually returned to Japan, but with a different perspective on the possibilities in life.

While he was in Kyoto visiting his family, Mino attended a casual gathering of Japanese elite society. A friend introduced him to Yoko Yamauchi, Hiroshi's daughter. The two of them were attracted to each other right away and soon fell in love. After meeting each other's families, and obtaining Hiroshi's permission, a wedding was planned. It was to be a big affair.

NEWLYWEDS

After the wedding, the young couple moved to Tokyo, where Yoko very much enjoyed the freedom from being away from the Nintendo business. She loved being married, and her husband was kind and attentive.

Unfortunately, the peaceful existence did not last. Marubeni, the large Japanese real estate developer that Mino worked for, constantly kept him away from home. His lengthy absences

ADVICE TO ASPIRING GAME DESIGNERS

Nintendo receives game ideas from aspiring designers every day, but it does not use them. Everything it creates is published in-house. On its Web site, the company offers advice for those interested in joining the Nintendo team some day: go to school, learn the trade, and then apply for a job. The site even recommends a specific school for aspiring designers: Digipen Institute of Technology located in Redmond, Washington, the same city as Nintendo of America's current headquarters.

Minoru Arakawa, 1992

frustrated Yoko, and she threatened to divorce
him if she was not allowed to join him on the next
project, which would be on the other side of the
world in Vancouver, Canada. The company president
eventually allowed her to move with her husband.

Life was not that much easier for Yoko in Vancouver. Marubeni's developments were struggling financially, and Mino was gone all the time, trying to turn things around. But at least her husband was not thousands of miles away. The couple also had a new baby girl, and Yoko struggled with the loneliness of caring for an infant by herself. In addition, she was still learning English, which made it difficult for her to feel a part of the community. She was getting homesick for Japan.

In 1979, after two years of living in Vancouver, Yoko and Mino went home to Japan for a visit. By this time, Yoko had given birth to another daughter. When

NINTENDO OF AMERICA'S LAWYER

Despite its humble beginnings, Nintendo of America (NOA) would go on to gain its grip on US culture with the advent of Donkey Kong arcade games, the Nintendo Entertainment System, Game Boy, and the Wii. However, this success came with its own problems. Lawsuits filed by companies competing for the entertainment dollar threw an occasional wrench into the works. Howard Lincoln was the US lawyer who helped NOA navigate through some very rough waters, in particular, a battle with Universal Studios, who claimed that Donkey Kong infringed on their King Kong film copyright. Nintendo had already licensed the game to several other companies, and a firestorm of fear was building: they could all potentially lose their investments through the legal fallout. Universal Studios lost the case since they did not in fact own the copyright; King Kong was in the public domain. Lincoln was eventually appointed the chairman of NOA in 1994. As of 2010, he was chief executive officer of the Seattle Mariners baseball team, which is owned by Hiroshi Yamauchi.

Yamauchi heard their story, he had a very direct talk with his son-in-law. He told Mino he should leave Marubeni and work for Nintendo, setting up a new operation in Malaysia, an island country in Southeast Asia.

Yoko was passionately against the idea of her husband working for her father. She had seen firsthand how brutally competitive life at Nintendo could be and the toll it had taken on her own family life. Mino turned down the offer and continued working for Marubeni in Vancouver. Yamauchi eventually dropped the Malaysia idea, but he still wanted to involve his son-in-law in the family business.

Yamauchi kept close tabs on how Mino was progressing at Marubeni, and he remained impressed with his son-in-law's managerial skills and determination. In addition to his strong work ethic, Mino was independent. He insisted that neither he nor Yoko accept any money from their wealthy families, even as they struggled. They had a tight budget, and when they moved from one home to another as renters, they packed their own things and did the moving themselves. When the real estate units his company developed were ready to sell, Mino served as a sales agent, and Yoko helped.

FINDING A WAY TO THE UNITED STATES

By the late 1970s, Yamauchi desperately wanted to expand his company in the United States, and he was convinced that Mino was the best man to head operations there. Yoko remained firmly against it, but Yamauchi worked on his son-in-law, who finally accepted a job offer. Yamauchi believed that Mino's experience in the United States was critical to Nintendo's success there. And, as a member of the Yamauchi family with the right skills, Mino was simply the best candidate. Mino became excited about the idea of starting the US branch of Nintendo. He discussed it with his wife, who recognized his desire to take the job. She was unsure, but Nintendo's new enterprise in the United States was definitely on.

Yoko and Mino opened the first Nintendo of America (NOA) office in New York in 1980, after traveling from Vancouver in a car filled with their belongings. They rented a place nearby in New Jersey, still using all of their own money. The first office the new branch rented was a small one, on Twenty-Fifth Street and Broadway, in Manhattan. Yoko was at work the first day, overseeing the deliveries of office equipment. +

The first Nintendo of America branch was located in Manhattan.

Kids playing arcade games in Los Angeles, California, in 1982

ENTER SHIGERU
MIYAMOTO

I n the 1980s, the fledgling NOA was trying
to break into the country's arcade business.
Nintendo had already been successful
creating arcade games for kids in Japan, including
Radarscope, Wild Gunman, Hellfire, and Sky

Skipper. To succeed, Yoko and Mino had to understand what kinds of games were making the most money in the United States. The couple spent long hours in arcades, watching kids play the games. The Arakawas eventually hired groups of kids and young adults to come to their warehouse, where they paid them to test arcade games of all kinds. The couple also hired a sales staff who convinced hotel and bar managers to let them set up Nintendo arcade games in their lobbies and lounges.

However, NOA was still struggling to get a start. It did not help that Yoko and Mino had begun their US launch in the midst of an overall collapse of the video game industry in the United States. No one was buying video games anymore. Would Nintendo products even get a chance in this climate?

Mino ordered a large shipment of Radarscope games from Japan, but they took months to arrive in New York. He was deeply worried that the buzz he and his sales team had been able to create around the company would fade before it even got a chance. All video game sales were slow, but Radarscope had done well in Japan and was expected to do just as well for Nintendo in the United States.

THE RADARSCOPE DISASTER

When Radarscope finally arrived, Mino's test gamers had bad news for him: the game was a bore. Other games similar to it were better. The sales staff was not able to sell it, even when the price was drastically reduced. Without any other hot games on the shelf, NOA was on the brink of complete failure. They had thousands of Radarscope arcade units doing nothing in their warehouse.

RADARSCOPE

The game Radarscope is often compared to Space Invaders, another Japanese-made arcade game. In Radarscope, a spaceship moved horizontally at the bottom of the screen. Players shot at a series of alien spaceships that appeared at the top. One explanation for the failure of Radarscope was its annoying, high-pitched sound effects.

Yamauchi was angry, and he blamed Mino. He said the large order of Radarscope games was the cause, not the game itself. Mino thought otherwise. He knew that only a different game would turn this NOA failure into a success.

However, Mino did reconsider the location of the NOA office. Shipping Japanese games to New York took months, but shipping goods to the West Coast would take significantly less time, as goods would need to cross only the Pacific Ocean and not entire continents. Both Yoko and Mino liked the idea of returning West, so they scoped out several spots before deciding on Seattle, Washington, where goods from Osaka, Japan, could arrive by boat in about a week.

They rented a 60,000 square-foot (18,288 sq m) warehouse and office space in the Seattle suburb of Tukwila. The NOA sales staff continued to sell other Nintendo games, and the Radarscopes were shipped from New York to their new location. They hoped Radarscope would eventually catch on, but Mino still wanted a new game from Japan.

Mino contacted Yamauchi again, who was less than understanding. Why should he risk losing more on this enterprise? Besides, NOA was such a small part of the company. But Yamauchi came around. He would let a designer create a new game for NOA. Yamauchi found just the right person for the job—the brilliant, young apprentice, Shigeru Miyamoto.

MIYAMOTO ON DECK

What makes a brilliant and creative video game designer? In the case of Nintendo designer Miyamoto, the answer to this question may lie in his childhood.

Miyamoto grew up in the 1960s. He lived in the country outside of Kyoto. His home felt far away from the noise and crowds of the nearby city. Without a television in his home, or even a family car that could potentially bring him into town for a bit of diversion, he had to find creative ways to entertain himself during long afternoons when he was not in school.

Miyamoto enjoyed roaming around the open rice fields near his home after the harvest season, climbing into mysterious caves in the woods to test his boyish nerve. His family brought him to Japanese Noh plays and puppet shows, which he loved. His creativity blossomed in this environment, and he discovered his gift for drawing. He also created hand-painted puppets for plays he had written and produced. There seemed to be no end to his ideas.

Creating art was extremely important to Miyamoto, to the point where he did not seem interested in much else. He tended to daydream through his lessons and avoided studying, in favor of

CHILDHOOD

Miyamoto draws directly from his childhood experiences when he creates his games. He explained, "The setting for games like Super Mario Brothers . . . comes directly from the mountains like Komugiyama and Tenjinyama. I scrambled around . . . their peaks and down their slopes, detective badge pinned to my shirt as I searched for caves."[1]

making toys out of wood, plastic, and metal. When he went off to college in the 1970s, his habits for avoiding his studies continued. Even though he was developing his skills as an artist at the Kanazawa Munici College of Industrial Arts and Crafts, he had a poor attendance record. He seemed unable to pull himself away from his group of cartoonist friends and other artistic activities, including playing bluegrass music on the guitar. He eventually graduated, but then it was time for the real world: he had to get a job.

Yamauchi was a friend of Miyamoto's father, so Miyamoto's father was able to arrange a job interview for his son with the successful businessman. Yamauchi granted the

MIYAMOTO'S PASSION

In a 2007 interview with CNN, Miyamoto explained what he loves about working with Nintendo and how it differs from other video game creators,

I have enjoyed creating something that is unique, something others have not done. I enjoy thinking about ways to create something that other people have not even thought about, something no one has managed to achieve. I often get inspiration from seeing the reaction from users playing games like Super Mario. For instance, I enjoyed making 3D versions of Super Mario 64 or Zelda.

My staff and I are motivated not by trying to out-sell whatever happens to be in the market, but rather trying to develop something that is totally unique. I think it's important that we enjoy that process. To create a new standard, you have to be up for that challenge and really enjoy it. This is the way we work and have done so many times.[2]

ADVICE FROM MIYAMOTO

When Miyamoto was once asked about what kind of advice he would give to aspiring video game designers, he said, "The most important thing is to create—when I was young, I made comics and puppets. Then take those creations and show them to people so you get feedback. Whether it is positive feedback or even if they make fun of it, repeating that process is a good thing for being prepared to make games."[3]

interview out of simple courtesy to his friend—the company head was not looking for what Miyamoto had to offer, or so he believed at first. The interview went well, so Yamauchi asked Miyamoto to come back for a second meeting and bring his ideas for some toys.

At the second meeting, Yamauchi listened quietly as Miyamoto presented his artwork and ideas, which included an array of brightly painted clothes hangers for children, in animal themes carved from wood. The wheels began to turn in Yamauchi's mind as he watched the young Miyamoto describe his creations and drawings. Miyamoto was hired that day as a Nintendo staff artist, the first and only one in the organization, but he would first work as an apprentice to one of the designers. +

Shigeru Miyamoto, 1992

CHAPTER 7

Donkey Kong was NOA's first successful arcade game.

DONKEY KONG ARRIVES

In 1980, Miyamoto got his first big break. With Nintendo's other video game developers busy with other projects, Yamauchi asked Miyamoto to create a game to replace Radarscope. This was a perfect fit for the new apprentice, because he loved the lively cartoon action of video games. He gladly accepted the challenge.

Perhaps thinking of his childhood experiences with theater, Miyamoto told Yamauchi that video games could be so much more than the simplistic "shoot-'em-ups" now on the market. He suggested deeper themes from fiction, using mythical characters.

Yamauchi was concerned less with artistic themes than turning a losing enterprise around. Radarscope had been a complete failure. He told Miyamoto that his assignment was to convert the failed Radarscope game into a product that would actually sell. Yokoi would be his boss.

Miyamoto got right to work and eventually came up with a theme he liked based on the US cartoon *Popeye*. Problems arose with licensing agreements, however. The cartoon's creators were reluctant to have their characters used in Nintendo's video game. Miyamoto had to drop the idea—or base it more loosely on the cartoon. Miyamoto combined his original idea with the King Kong story from the legendary gorilla monster film. He began with a gorilla that was not nearly as dangerous as King Kong. He added a little man and decided that the gorilla would be his enormous pet.

The gorilla, Miyamoto thought, should not be happy with that arrangement. The gorilla finds being the pet of such an insignificant little man to be humiliating. He kidnaps the man's girlfriend to even the score.

Miyamoto and his team first decided that the little man would be a carpenter, but later they decided he was a plumber. Technology of the time limited the details of the game's graphics. The plumber was dressed in bright blue overalls and a red hat to make him easy to see on the screen. Miyamoto also gave him large, blue cartoon eyes and a bushy moustache that would make it easier to see his nose.

The artist devised the plumber's role in the game, which was to rescue his girlfriend from the naughty gorilla. Naturally, the gorilla was nearly impossible to catch. The creature climbed atop buildings with the girl, just as in the King Kong movies. The plumber climbed up ramps and ladders to get to the top of a building, while the gorilla heaved barrels and lumber over the side to crush him.

Miyamoto wrote the music accompaniment himself. But the game's name required a bit of research.

NAMING THE GAME

Since he had based the story loosely on King Kong, Miyamoto wanted to include the name Kong right from the start. Everyone would associate the name with a gorilla. His gorilla also had a severe stubborn streak and was a bit goofy, so, after some discussion, he and the designers added donkey to the name. *Don-key* in Japanese means silly, goofy, or even stupid. The plumber would be named Jumpman. At last, Miyamoto was ready to send out the game to replace Radarscope. Donkey Kong was on its way to NOA's new headquarters in Seattle.

JUMPMAN AND DONKEY KONG

When Miyamoto's game Donkey Kong arrived in Seattle in 1981, the sales staff tried it out and instantly hated it. What did the

TOP SELLERS

Donkey Kong's original success was continued by Nintendo's Super Mario Brothers video game, which came out in 1985. This was the best-selling game of all time for many years, with more than 40 million copies sold. But as of 2010, it had been bumped down to second place. Which game was in first place? Wii Sports, with more than 41 million games sold.

MARIO TURNS 25

The arcade version of Donkey Kong went on to evolve into the Super Mario Brothers game for the Nintendo Entertainment System (NES) in 1985. For the twenty-fifth anniversary of Super Mario, Nintendo posted an image that linked all the different versions of Mario over the years, from the blocky-looking little smudge that bounced around the screen in the arcade version to the sleek animated guy he is today.

name Donkey Kong even mean? But when a game tester named Howard Phillips—a young man— tried it in the warehouse, he had to be dragged away. Still, Mino Arakawa called Yamauchi to complain about the name, but he insisted on leaving it just like it was. "It is a good game," Yamauchi said.[1]

When Donkey Kong was activated, the story introduced the overall theme of the game, but it was all in Japanese. All the character's names had to be changed to English ones. Arakawa knew the name Jumpman was not going to go over well, and he named the princess Pauline, after a Nintendo salesman's wife. Just as they were trying to figure out a name for the little plumber, someone knocked on the warehouse door.

Arakawa answered it. It was the landlord, who yelled at

Arakawa in front of everyone for not paying the rent.
The landlord's name was Mario Segale. Arakawa
reassured his landlord that he would be paid, and the
man left. The landlord's name, however—Mario—
stuck in Arakawa's mind. The group decided that
Super Mario would be a great replacement name for
Jumpman.

LAUNCHING DONKEY KONG

In the summer of
1981, a tavern near the
Nintendo warehouse
allowed a salesman to
set up Donkey Kong,
and the game was
practically an overnight
success. People were
lining up inside the
bar to play the coin-
operated arcade game.
Yamauchi's instincts
had been right again.
The young apprentice,
Miyamoto, had never
designed a game before,

HOWARD PHILLIPS

Soon after NOA's move to Seattle, an advertisement was placed in the *Seattle Times*, which read: "Have fun and play games for a living." Howard Phillips, a 20-year-old red-haired gaming enthusiast, answered the advertisement and became the company's fifth employee, eventually handling all shipping during the first years of NOA's run with the coin-operated Donkey Kong.

Phillips loved games, and his feedback about the games gained him the trust of NOA upper-level managers. In 1989, he was promoted to director of Game Creative at Nintendo, but Arakawa always referred to him simply as the "Game Master." He also worked as an editor for *Nintendo Power*. In 1991, Phillips left the company to work for LucasArts, a video game creator.

and yet he had created what would prove to be the most successful Nintendo game yet. Of the 3,000 Radarscope arcade games shipped to the United States from Japan, 2,000 were converted to Donkey Kong games and sold. Arakawa ordered thousands more. By June 1982, approximately 60,000 games were sold and NOA had made $180 million in sales from Donkey Kong. +

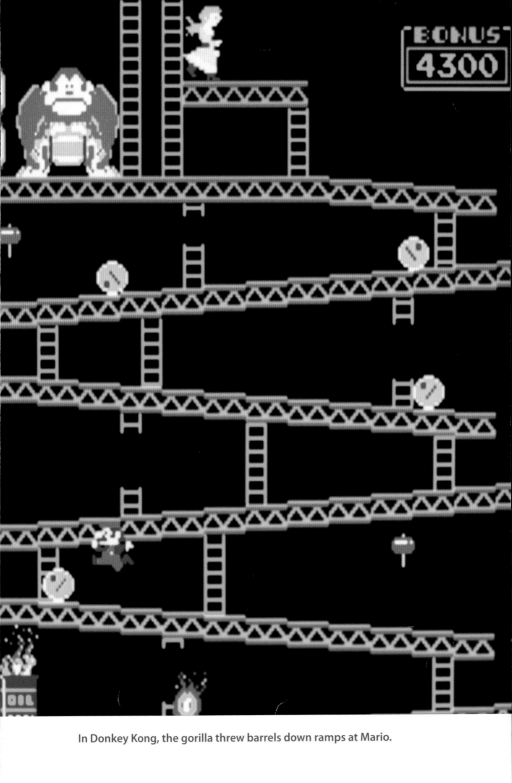

In Donkey Kong, the gorilla threw barrels down ramps at Mario.

Atari 2600 had a joystick and switches.

BRINGING VIDEO GAMES HOME

With the successful arcade games in Japan and the United States, as well as the success of a few home video games, Nintendo turned its attention to home video games exclusively. In the early 1980s, there were already a variety of home game systems on the market in the United States and Japan, such as the Atari 2600, Colecovision, and Magnavox Odyssey. Some video game systems came with a certain number of games on the machine. No games could be added to these systems. Other video game systems were cartridge-style. With these systems, players could insert cartridges of different games into the machine to play them. When players got sick of a game, they could purchase a new one.

A significant problem with these video game systems was that their designs could be easily copied, which made them vulnerable to poor quality imitators. Additionally, designers could create games to be used in cartridge game systems whether or not they were affiliated with the company that produced the console. However, cheap games often reflected badly on the system's creators rather than the company that created the game.

Yamauchi's new orders for engineer Masayuki Uemura were to create a cartridge game system so unique that another company could not figure out a way to copy it any time soon. He said, "It must be so much better that there will be no question which system the customers will want."[1] It also had to be affordable, and this proved to be the biggest challenge for the developers. Yamauchi wanted the cartridge system to sell for $75. This was at least $100 less than the competitor's systems already on the market.

Uemura put his inquisitive nature to work researching competitor's games. He determined that most systems had interesting graphics, but the games lacked action. Uemura also decided that the quality of the animation and the overall pacing of the games could be improved. However, all of these improvements would mean adding an expensive high-speed microprocessor. This would drive the price up much higher than the $75 limit.

ARCADES

Uemura turned to arcade games for answers. Nintendo's arcade systems already had a way of completely engaging players. What were the keys to their success? Uemura figured out that quickness and mental challenge were the two main components of a game that kept players fully interested. However, making that happen in a console-sized unit would not be possible without the more expensive microprocessors. Days of intense experiments were conducted among Nintendo's arcade engineers and programmers, but in the end they determined they would have to purchase faster processors to improve the speed of play.

YAMAUCHI'S MOVES

When Uemura approached Ricoh Electronics, a company that manufactured processors, about the project, they scoffed at the price Nintendo was willing to pay. It was nowhere near enough. However, they changed their minds when Yamauchi made an audacious promise: he would order 3 million units over a two-year period.

Word around Nintendo was that Yamauchi's giant order

ARCADES IN JAPAN

Although the popularity of arcades in the United States has greatly waned, arcades are still popular in most big Japanese cities. A young US journalist, Brian Ashcraft, has chronicled this cultural phenomenon in his book, *Arcade Mania: The Turbo-Charged World of Japan's Game Centers*.

Ashcraft was still in the United States when arcades began to decline, so coming to Japan was like "being in arcade heaven," he says, where arcades are just another part of the urban environment. "Arcades are very much integrated into the Japanese urban landscape. . . . Some players often practice in their neighborhood game center and get amazingly good before daring to play and show off at famous arcades in Tokyo."[2]

Ashcraft explains that gamers show a level of respect for each other in the arcades. He writes, "Japanese arcades are, in a way, an extension of Japanese society. . . . Japanese manners extend into arcades. Things that are considered polite and respectful in Japanese society at large carry over into arcades."[3]

Japan is a small country, and real estate is extremely expensive in crowded cities like Tokyo. Instead of having arcades spread out over large areas, Tokyo arcade owners save money by using less space on the ground. They build their arcades high instead.

Arcades were very popular in Japan.

for Ricoh processors was crazy. The games and system had not even been proven on the market, and besides, the company had never sold that many of any of their products. However, Yamauchi was thinking much further into the future for his company and its game cartridge system. He wanted it to succeed in the long term, and acquiring the key processing components at the right price was a way to keep the costs competitively low from the start.

He made sure an additional circuit was added that could accommodate additions down the road, such as a modem, for connection to the Internet via a phone line, or a keyboard, if a customer wanted that capability. This addition would later be referred to as Nintendo's Trojan Horse, because this deceptively simple addition was a built-in link to future sales.

Nintendo Family Computer (Famicom) and its interchangeable game cartridges were released in 1983, and Nintendo sold approximately 500,000 units in Japan in the first two months. Famicoms were equipped with something no other systems had at the time: a joy pad, or controller. All other consoles used a joystick. Controllers were easier to use than joysticks since they did not require high levels of force. They were very simple: two fire buttons and a Start and Select button in the center.

However, a glitch in one of the computer chips was causing the system to freeze up. Not wanting

JOYSTICKS

Joysticks are associated with video games, but the term originally comes from the military. A joystick is the central controlling unit of an aircraft; moving it in different directions will cause the aircraft to respond. As in an aircraft, video game joysticks are attached to a solid base, and when pressure is applied in one direction or another (or when its buttons are pressed), there is a response in the game action. Joystick controls are also used on arcade games.

to risk his long-term vision of success for the system,
Yamauchi made another big move; he ordered a
complete recall of all systems rather than fix the
broken ones as they were returned.

Now that the defective chip was gone and
replaced with one that worked, the Famicom was free
to climb to dizzying heights of popularity in Japan.
The system owners soon demanded more games.
With a functioning and popular video game system
in Japan, Yamauchi now could see an opportunity to
bring a new game system to the United States as well. +

Children in Tokyo playing with the Famicom

NOA released the Nintendo Entertainment System
as a US version of Famicom.

NINTENDO OF
AMERICA EXPANDS

As the Donkey Kong arcade games brought in more profits, NOA expanded, creating new games for the arcades. Games with titles such as Donkey Kong Junior and Punch Out emerged, to name a few. The company also released a new type of arcade game that allowed two players to play at the same time, called the VS for *versus*. The Famicom video game system also continued to sell very well in Japan, but most of Nintendo's business in the United States was based on the coin-operated arcade games.

Yamauchi wanted a bigger slice of the US video game market. He told Arakawa that he wanted to launch a US version of Famicom. However, the home video game business in the United States was barely breathing. Game manufacturers had flooded the market, and many of the games were poorly produced. Video game systems did not have control over who made the games for their systems, so it was hard for consumers to tell good games from bad ones. If a game was bad, it could not be returned. The US video game market collapsed in 1983, and consumers moved on to other forms of entertainment.

TWIN FAMICOM

Sharp electronics was Nintendo's partner in hardware products, and in 1986, Sharp released the Twin Famicom, licensed by Nintendo. Like the Famicom, it was essentially a computer, but it combined the Famicom Disk System (FDS) with the Famicom game console. The disk system allowed players to store game data on separate floppy disks. The system was sold only in Japan.

NINTENDO POWER

Video game play is not always straightforward. Cheats, tricks, and strategies can make all the difference in a player's ability to achieve the next level of play. *Nintendo Power* magazine was created for avid players looking for ways to beat Nintendo games. The magazine's information came straight from the source: Nintendo game developers. The magazine started as a newsletter called *Nintendo Fun Club*. In 1988, it became *Nintendo Power*. The magazine was published in-house for 20 years by NOA before being published by an outside company.

COMPETITORS BECOME PARTNERS

Nintendo was not going to give up on the US consumer's once-blossoming interest in video games. At first, the company worked with the established video game manufacturer, Atari, by licensing Donkey Kong for the company's home computers. Nintendo executives also tried to set up a market through Atari for the Famicom, but this fizzled. It turned out that the Famicom would have to sink or swim on its own in the United States.

Back in Japan, Yokoi's team had created the Robotic Operating Buddy (ROB), a small robot controlled by the Famicom video game system. Arakawa loved the product, but in test trials, kids hated it. Yamauchi ignored the reactions and told him to sell the ROB in only New York City, just to see what would happen. Sales were not great. However, the US public slowly began to show interest in video games again.

NINTENDO ENTERTAINMENT SYSTEM

In 1985, NOA decided the time was right to release the US version of Nintendo's Famicom— the Nintendo Entertainment System (NES) and its package of games. The first NES design was released in two different packages: the Control Deck and the Deluxe Set. The system for both packages was the same, but they came with different games. The Deluxe Set had the console, two controllers, the ROB, a Zapper Gun, and two games: Gyromite and Duck Hunt. The Control Deck had a console, two controllers, and a set of Super Mario Brothers games.

The NES was officially released in New York on October 18, 1985, when the first shipment arrived with 100,000 systems. Sales were very good over the holiday season, so Nintendo test-marketed Los Angeles in February of the following year. After that, they test-marketed Chicago and San Francisco, and eventually, launched the products nationwide in February 1986. Nintendo also made a distribution arrangement with toy companies, which increased

ALL ABOUT MARIO

Mario first appeared in the Donkey Kong arcade game, but Miyamoto later expanded the character in Donkey Kong Jr., where Mario played a villain. Miyamoto also invented games that led Mario through plumber-related places: sewers with strange insects and sea critters. For the two-player game version, Miyamoto added a brother for the second player, Mario's twin brother named Luigi.

But Mario became famous in the Mario Brothers games. In Mario Brothers, Mario and Luigi investigate pesky critters in New York sewers. In Super Mario Brothers, the two characters return to fight villains in a new land called Mushroom Kingdom, with its own royalty, Princess Peach. In the games that followed, the brothers would increase in size and power as they conquered enemies. Finding coins gave them extra lives, giving them more time to solve the problems of hidden and blocked-off rooms.

Super Mario was released as a part of the NES in 1985, which included the whimsical but slightly scary Bowser, and large pits of lava—challenges that Mario must overcome in Mushroom Kingdom to rescue Princess Peach.

the number of outlets for its products.

THE NES AROUND THE WORLD

The world release of the NES came in stages. Most European countries received it in 1986. England, Ireland, Italy, Australia, and New Zealand received it in 1987 through a Mattel distributorship. Europeans did not find the NES as captivating as other countries had. Sega had already released a successful video game system called the Master System in Europe, which many found superior to the NES.

Many Europeans were also more interested in computer games than video game consoles. Nintendo's system outsold Sega's product in Australia, but by much less than in the United States.

KEYS TO SUCCESS

With the success of the NES in 1985, Nintendo has been credited for reviving the video game market in the United States. Knowing it was entering a tough market, Nintendo had promised retailers it would buy back unsold stock, which helped stores feel more comfortable selling Nintendo products in the unstable market. Aware of the problem it faced in convincing reluctant consumers, Nintendo had made the NES a little different than other systems of the time. It had a front-loading system of cartridges resembling the familiar-looking home VCRs.

MUSHROOM WORLDS

Initially, Mario spent time in Mushroom Kingdom, a fantasy world he shared with his brother, Luigi, and Princess Toadstool (later known as Princess Peach), Mario's girlfriend. Mushrooms are a source of strength for Mario. When he eats a "super" mushroom, his body and strength grow. Some people have pointed out that eating mushrooms to grow bigger also happens in the book *Alice's Adventures in Wonderland*. However, Miyamoto denies the similarities.

Later versions of the game expanded the concept to Mushroom World, which has different lands and inhabitants, including humans, toads, and small turtle-like animals called Koopas. One of the most famous Koopas is Bowser, also known as King Koopa. Bowser tries to capture Princess Peach and conquer Mario's Mushroom Kingdom.

MARIO MEDIA

The little plumber Mario has inspired some big things in the entertainment business. A movie based on the game starred Academy Award-winning British actor Bob Hoskins as Mario. The live-action film entitled *Super Mario Bros.* was released in 1993. The film received bad reviews and did poorly at the box office, but it was also nominated for two Saturn Awards for best costume and best makeup. Mario has also inspired a comic book series, a television cartoon show, and a rock opera.

Nintendo also learned from other video game manufacturer's mistakes. Unauthorized, cheaply produced games could not work on their system because of their unique 10NES lockout chip. They also created the Nintendo Seal of Quality, making authenticity easily recognizable on the label. Faith in the video game products was restored, and the competition with other manufacturers began again.

By the end of 1985, Nintendo had sold more than 1 million units in the United States. It would eventually sell nearly 62 million units, and the NES would become the best-selling video game system in the United States until the Wii. Meanwhile, Nintendo kept producing one successful game after another. Nintendo had kicked the video game door wide open. The United States provided the biggest video game market in the world, and Nintendo had captured it through innovation. With Yamauchi at the helm, it seemed there was no end in sight. +

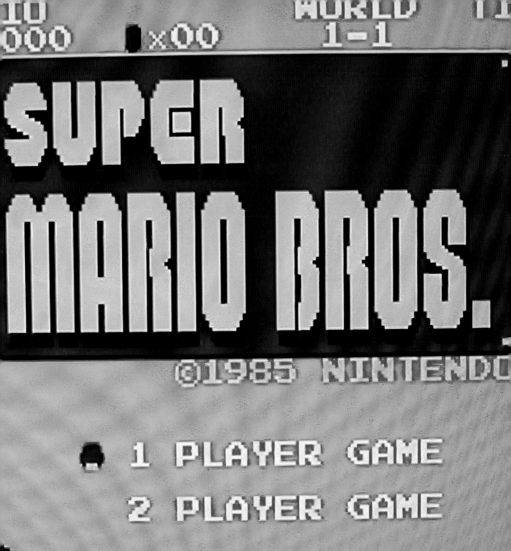

Super Mario Brothers was one of many popular games for the NES.

Nintendo DS

THE SKY IS NOT
THE LIMIT

T he NES was just the beginning in video game
systems for Nintendo. The next big Nintendo
launch was the Family Computer System Disk
in 1986 in Japan. This was followed by the handheld
Game Boy in 1989. The competition had released

handhelds with complex forms of operation and play. Game Boy was different. Its simple design made it approachable by anyone, not only highly skilled gamers. The handheld system combined the Game and Watch with the NES concept: interchangeable game cartridges, yet small enough to hold in your hands. Similar to the NES, Game Boy hardware would set up a huge market for interchangeable game software. It also had a long battery life. Kids loved the Game Boy, but it was also popular among adults. Two hundred thousand were sold in Japan in two weeks, and 40,000 were sold the first day they were launched in the United States.

Meanwhile, the famed Nintendo Research and Development Team 4 headed by Miyamoto was "retired" in 1989. The Entertainment Analysis and Development (EAD) division took its place and became the largest

WARIO

Developers at Nintendo decided that Mario should have another antagonist besides Bowser and Donkey Kong, so they invented Wario. He first appeared in the 1992 Game Boy game, Super Mario Land. He had an exaggerated resemblance to Mario. The name Wario is derived from Mario, and also from the Japanese adjective *warui*, which means "bad," suggesting that he is a bad version of Mario.

POKEMON SERIES FOR GAME BOY

Pokemon games for Game Boy, and later N64, were developed by Game Freak, which creates games exclusively for Nintendo and Creatures Inc., a Nintendo subsidiary. The games were released for the first time in Japan in 1996 for the Game Boy, and they all have a consistent form of play in which players can first choose from three Pokemon characters: a grass type, a fire type, or a water type. Pokemon Yellow varies from this theme, where a Pikachu character is provided. Throughout the game, the player can use his or her starting Pokemon to catch and train more Pokemon characters. The success of the game led to the famous Pokemon playing cards, a television show, comics, and movies.

division in the company. Miyamoto and Takashi Tezuka took the lead of this department.

MORE VIDEO GAME SYSTEMS

As the 1990s dawned, Nintendo continued to produce new systems it hoped would be competitive in the growing industry. A new system called the Super Nintendo Entertainment System came out in 1990. In 1996, the company launched the popular Nintendo 64 (N64), and in 1998, came Game Boy Color. This was followed by the 2001 Game Boy Advance, and the GameCube, a home video game system that followed the new trend of using discs instead of cartridges.

STRUGGLING TO COMPETE

Although the company released several new products, Nintendo struggled in the late 1990s and early 2000s. The release of N64

Nintendo 64 was released in 1996.

in 1996 saw sales that lagged behind Sony's more popular PlayStation. N64 was able to capitalize on the success of popular Pokemon characters by releasing several games that featured them— Pokemon Snap and Pokemon Stadium—for N64. Still, N64 was not the well-selling console it was hoped to be. Buyers seemed more drawn to PlayStation and its games.

In 2001, Nintendo had another struggle with the release of the GameCube. Released in the same year as Microsoft's Xbox and Sony's PlayStation 2, the GameCube struggled to attract buyers.

Xbox won more buyers due to its online gaming capability, which neither the GameCube nor PlayStation 2 had.

Nintendo had lost its strength in the video game industry. It would have to do something drastic, and reach a new market, to rise again. As plans for the Wii were underway, many people felt it was one last desperate attempt for Nintendo to gain back buyers that would immediately end in failure. But, in fact, the Wii's unique use of movement would appeal to more than the common video game player. Unlike other systems that were mainly marketed toward kids, the Wii appealed to people of all ages. The Wii would help Nintendo reclaim its position at the top of the electronic gaming industry.

HANDHELD SYSTEMS

Handheld systems continued to be a hot trend in games for Nintendo. Nintendo released a new handheld version in 2004—the Nintendo DS. The Nintendo DS had two screens with a microphone and touch screen capability. The Nintendo DS evolved, and the company released two new handheld systems: the DS Lite, which was released in 2006, followed by the DSi, in 2009. The DSi

has two lenses that allow players
to take pictures of themselves and
the people around them while they
play. The DS Lite and DSi are
rectangular shaped and lightweight.
They are also equipped with
microphones and touch screens
that allow manipulation of photos.
Both systems are small computers
that are also powerful enough for
fast-action game play. The DSi has
a built-in Web browser and Wi-Fi
capabilities, so players can join in
play with other gamers at home or
around the world. Or they can surf
the Internet.

A NEW COMPANY PRESIDENT

Yamauchi finally stepped down
as the company's third president
in 2002. He was replaced by
Satoru Iwata, who had started as
a programmer at the Nintendo
subsidiary HAL laboratories
(named after the computer "Hal"

YAMAUCHI IN RETIREMENT

Now the richest man in Japan, Hiroshi Yamauchi spends his days at his home, which is located near the majestic Buddhist Shogoin temple. But even though he is retired, he still receives messages about the company and has a lot of influence over the management. Iwata, the company president since May of 2002, says, "He really is amazing. His instincts are incredibly keen, and he asks these piercing questions—you think to yourself, how did he know? I talk to him every so often on the phone, and it's like he could come back tomorrow and be the president without any trouble, he's that sharp."[1]

GAME SHIFT

The success of the video game industry appeared to peak in the last years of the twentieth century. Games were becoming more complex and the software development more costly. At a 2000 conference, Yamauchi explained his opinion to industry analysts that complex, costly game systems were not good for the video game industry. The shift that Nintendo needed did not come along until Iwata took over the company in 2002. The company rebounded with the success of its consumer-friendly, mainstream products such as Brain Age, the Wii, and the DS.

from the futuristic film *2001 Space Odyssey*). As a graduate of Tokyo's Institute of Technology, Iwata had the right background for Nintendo's high-tech game development. He helped create Kirby games, among others. He also played an important role in shaping the strategy of the GameCube. In 2000, he became the company's head of corporate planning. Iwata was the first Nintendo president who was not related to the Yamauchi family by birth or through marriage.

Things changed a little at Nintendo when Iwata became company president. During the Yamauchi years, only a few people were allowed to speak to the company president. The Iwata era was different, because Iwata spoke directly with employees, explaining business objectives personally. When asked what was different about Nintendo without its former leader, Miyamoto said that the company's direction used to be set by one person at the top, which created what he described as a somewhat "stuffy" company atmosphere. "But Iwata coming in with his outsider's perspective improved the ventilation, so to speak," he said.[2] Iwata has refused to rest on the company laurels. Like Yamauchi and Arakawa, he knows that the way to keep the company going strong is with new, creative, and interesting games. New games for the DS handheld system called Brain Age and Nintendogs were both a big success in the early 2000s. The DS systems' releases also increased the company's sales; nearly 2 million were sold in Japan in late 2008. The DSi, released in Japan on November 1, 2008, made up 1.66 million of those sales.

NEW FOR THE WII

As of 2010, the Wii was the best-selling video game console ever made. When Nintendo introduced the Wii in 2006, it had several new features including the motion-sensitive remote control and built-in Wi-Fi. In 2010, the newly introduced Wii Sports game inspired a real-life event—the Wii Olympics. Nintendo hosted its own 2010 Summer Olympic Games with players competing in hula hoop contests on the Wii Fit Plus, basketball and bowling on Wii Sports Resort, the New Super Mario Bros Wii, and Mario Kart Wii.

Tournaments were held at Six Flags theme parks in Texas, New Jersey, Georgia, and other states, in addition to shopping malls across the country. "The Wii Games: Summer 2010 events are a celebration of the fun, active, inclusive spirit of Wii," said Cammie Dunaway, NOA's executive vice president of Sales and Marketing.[3]

Nintendo has sold more than 70 million Wii's since its launch. Around half of those were sold in the United States alone. This is striking when compared to Sony's PlayStation 3 (PS3) and Microsoft's Xbox 360, each having sold around 40 million systems as of 2010. Nintendo clearly dominates the market not only in the

INSPIRATION FOR WII FIT

Miyamoto and his team were in charge of creating the software for the Wii. The team first created two packs of games for the new console. They created the "Party Pack" for the whole family and the "Sports Pack," which had games based on sports. These became Wii Play and Wii Sports respectively.

Around this time, Miyamoto had just turned 40 years old, and he decided to work out to lose some weight. He noticed that swimming made the weight come off naturally, and he enjoyed getting in shape. He knew that people wanted to have fun while losing weight. Through this process, he decided to create the Wii "Health Pack," which became Wii Fit. By late December of 2008, the company had sold 14 million Wii Fit games around the world.

United States and Japan, but all over the world. A technology reporter for *GamePro* magazine wrote,

> *Basically, Nintendo has what the two other console manufacturers would give their right analog sticks to possess: a large presence in the homes of average consumers as well as a stranglehold on the public's perception of what a "video game" is.*[4]

WHAT IS NEXT?

In June 2009, reporters asked Iwata what new ideas to expect from Nintendo in the following year. He explained that the company would focus on games that pick up where other games such as Brain Age and Wii Fit had left off. Behind him was an image of something called the Wii Vitality Sensor. Iwata said,

> *Just as we're able to sense the player's center of balance in the Wii Fit, we're now able to sense their internal state. Where previous games have only been sources of excitement and stimulation, now we'll be able to relieve stress and encourage better sleep.*[5]

A game called Wii Relax, expected to be packaged with the Wii Vitality Sensor, was in production as of 2010.

Despite producing new cutting-edge products, Nintendo continues to be a generally cautious company. In Osamu Inoue's book *Nintendo Magic*, he wrote,

> *Besides amusement and software orientation, at the heart of Nintendo's corporate culture is deep respect for the importance of luck. No matter how huge their hits might be, they are careful to stay humble.*[6]

Nintendo's success has been felt far beyond the shores of Japan. The company is credited with saving a dying video game industry in the United States with the NES in the mid-1980s. Once the market was firmly established, companies became licensed producers of compatible games, creating new jobs and a thrust of competition that generated new consoles and software in the United States and abroad.

NINTENDO WORLD

US citizens have felt a cultural impact from Nintendo's broad appeal to kids. Nielsen Media Research showed that in the early 1990s, more kids played video games on their Nintendo consoles than watched cartoons, even the popular

Nickelodeon channel. Kids also spent more time engaged with electronic gadgets than in school or with friends. When they were not playing with Nintendo gadgets, they were watching Nintendo cartoon shows, reading Nintendo magazines and books, drinking from Nintendo-themed mugs, and sleeping on Nintendo sheets. Parents and teachers became concerned about the effects and wondered if it had an impact on learning and social development.

Now more recognizable than Mickey Mouse among children, the popular Mario is seen by some as an invader. David Sheff, author of *Game Over*, writes, "Mickey's message: *We play fair and we work hard and we're in harmony . . .* Mario imparted other values: *Kill or be killed. Time is running out. You are on your own.*"[7]

But many point out that Mario and other Nintendo games

NEVER TOO OLD

In 2003, 50-year-old Miyamoto was asked if he was getting a bit old to be in the business of video games, which is largely considered a young person's domain. He said, "I don't feel like I'm too old. . . . I'm a Dracula-like person. Just like he was always trying to get his energy from the blood of young ladies, so I get energy by working with younger people."[8]

are more about entertainment than anything
else, and parents ultimately control the amount
of time kids spend on the systems. Additionally,
many of Nintendo's Wii games help generate social
connections, as well as entertain, and even promote
healthy living through exercise games. So who
knows? Nintendo may change the world yet again, to
be a more physically fit and socially engaged place. +

Satoru Iwata, 2010

TIMELINE

1889

Nintendo begins in Kyoto, Japan, as a business creating playing cards.

1907

Nintendo becomes the first Japanese company to manufacture Western-style playing cards.

1963

The company name is changed to Nintendo Company Ltd.

1966

The Ultra Hand appears on the market.

1977

Nintendo's first home video game system, the Color TV Game 6, is launched.

1927

Hiroshi Yamauchi is born on November 7.

1929

Fusajiro Yamauchi retires and appoints Sekiryo Yamauchi as the new president.

1949

Hiroshi Yamauchi becomes the third company president at the age of 21.

1980

The handheld system the Game and Watch is launched.

1980

Nintendo starts a branch in the United States.

1985

The Nintendo Entertainment System is released in the United States.

TIMELINE

1989	1990	1996
Game Boy is released.	The Super Nintendo Entertainment System is launched.	Nintendo 64 is launched.

2001	2002	2004
The GameCube is launched.	Yamauchi steps down as president. He is succeeded by Iwata.	Nintendo DS is released.

1998	2000	2001
Game Boy Color is launched.	Satoru Iwata is appointed head of Nintendo's Corporate Planning Division.	Game Boy Advance is released.

2006	2008	2009
The Wii is released and sells out almost immediately.	The Wii Fit is released in May.	The Nintendo DSi is released.

ESSENTIAL FACTS

CREATORS

Fusajiro Yamauchi (as playing card business), November 22, 1860

Hiroshi Yamauchi (as a video game business), November 7, 1927

DATE FOUNDED

1889

CHALLENGES

During the collapse of the US video game market, Minoru Arakawa faced challenges with bringing Nintendo to the United States as the first games promoted failed to capture attention. In the late 1990s and early 2000s, Nintendo struggled to release a video game system that would dominate in the competitive market.

SUCCESSES

Hiroshi Yamauchi's faith in creative minds helped Nintendo make a neat transition from card maker to high-tech entertainment giant. Nintendo's first advanced video game system, Famicom, sold approximately 500,000 units in Japan in only two months. Nintendo's US version of the Famicom, the Nintendo Entertainment System, became the best-selling video game system the United States had seen. The Wii later claimed this title.

IMPACT ON SOCIETY

Nintendo is considered responsible for reviving the US video game industry after it crashed in 1983. With the release of the Wii in 2006, Nintendo introduced a new kind of video game technology to the world.

QUOTE

"Throw away all your old ideas in order to come up with something new. We must look in different directions."
—*Hiroshi Yamauchi*

GLOSSARY

apprentice

Someone who works for another person in order to learn a skill or trade.

consensus

A majority opinion.

console

The control unit of a game system, containing memory and processors.

consumer

A person who utilizes economic goods; someone who spends money on products.

contender

One who struggles with an opponent.

innovation

An idea or thing that is new, different, or unexpected.

interaction

A mutual exchange.

kanji

A system of Japanese writing using symbols derived from Chinese writing.

microprocessor
An integrated computer circuit that processes all the
information in a computer.

retail
Selling directly to consumers.

semiconductors
Materials that allow the flow of electric current to happen in a
controlled way.

vitality
A life force and capacity for survival.

ADDITIONAL RESOURCES

SELECTED BIBLIOGRAPHY

Forster, Winnie. *The Encyclopedia of Game Machines.* Utting, Germany: Winnie Forster/Gameplan, 2005. Print.

Inoue, Osamu. *Nintendo Magic.* New York: Vertical, 2001. Print.

Kent, Stephen L. *The Ultimate History of Video Games.* New York: Random, 2001. Print.

Sheff, David. *Game Over: How Nintendo Zapped an American Industry, Captured Your Dollars, and Enslaved Your Children.* New York: Random, 1993. Print.

FURTHER READINGS

Burns, Jan. *Shigeru Miyamoto.* San Diego, CA: KidHaven, 2006. Print.

Hart, Christopher. *Manga Mania Video Games: How to Draw the Characters & Environments of Manga Video Games.* New York: Watson-Guptill, 2004. Print.

Pardew, Les. *Game Design for Teens.* Boston: Course Technology PTR, 2004. Print.

WEB LINKS

To learn more about Nintendo, visit ABDO Publishing Company online at **www.abdopublishing.com**. Web sites about Nintendo are featured on our Book Links page. These links are routinely monitored and updated to provide the most current information available.

PLACES TO VISIT

American Classic Arcade Museum
579 Endicott Street North, Laconia, NH 03246
http://www.classicarcademuseum.org
The American Classic Arcade Museum is dedicated to preserving the history of coin-operated arcade machines. Visitors to the museum can view, and even play, old arcade games.

National Museum of Play
One Manhattan Square, Rochester, NY 14607
585-263-2700
http://www.thestrong.org
The National Museum of Play exhibits old toys including video games, dolls, sports equipment, and books.

SOURCE NOTES

CHAPTER 1. WELCOMING THE WII

1. "The Big Ideas Behind Nintendo's Wii." *Next-Gen Game Consoles.* Bloomberg L.P. 16 Nov. 2006. Web. 28 Oct. 2001.

2. "Nintendo Wii Consumer Comments." *Nintendo Wii.* n.p. 29 Apr. 2006. Web. 27 Oct. 2010.

3. Chris Morris. "Nintendo Goes Wii." *CNNMoney.com.* Cable News Network. 27 Apr. 2006. Web. 28 Oct. 2010.

4. *WiiUniverse.info.* n.p. 2010. Web. 8 Nov. 2010.

5. "The Big Ideas Behind Nintendo's Wii." *Nest-Gen Game Consoles.* Bloomberg L.P. 16 Nov. 2006. Web. 28 Oct. 2001.

6. Ibid.

CHAPTER 2. PLAYING CARDS

None.

CHAPTER 3. HIROSHI YAMAUCHI RULES

1. David Sheff. *Game Over: How Nintendo Zapped an American Industry, Captured Your Dollars, and Enslaved Your Children.* New York: Random, 1993. Print. 21.

2. Ibid. 23.

CHAPTER 4. NEW TECHNOLOGY

1. David Sheff. *Game Over: How Nintendo Zapped an American Industry, Captured Your Dollars, and Enslaved Your Children.* New York: Random, 1993. Print. 28.
2. Ibid. 51.
3. Ibid. 58.

CHAPTER 5. NINTENDO BRANCHES OUT

None.

CHAPTER 6. ENTER SHIGERU MIYAMOTO

1. Osamu Inoue. *Nintendo Magic.* New York: Vertical Inc., 2001. Print. 63.
2. "Shigeru Miyamoto Talk Asia Interview." *CNN World.* Cable News Network. 14 Feb. 2007. Web. 1 Nov. 2010.
3. "10 Questions for Shigeru Miyamoto." *Time.* Time Inc. 19 Jul. 2007. Web. 28 Oct. 2010.

SOURCE NOTES CONTINUED

CHAPTER 7. DONKEY KONG ARRIVES

1. David Sheff. *Game Over: How Nintendo Zapped an American Industry, Captured Your Dollars, and Enslaved Your Children.* New York: Random, 1993. Print. 109.

CHAPTER 8. BRINGING VIDEO GAMES HOME

1. David Sheff. *Game Over: How Nintendo Zapped an American Industry, Captured Your Dollars, and Enslaved Your Children.* New York: Random, 1993. Print. 29.

2. Victor Godinez. "American Gamer Chronicles Japan's Vibrant Arcade Culture in Book." *PhysOrg.com.* PhysOrg.com. 20 Jan. 2009. Web. 8 Nov. 2010.

3. Ibid.

CHAPTER 9. NINTENDO OF AMERICA EXPANDS

None.

CHAPTER 10. THE SKY IS NOT THE LIMIT

1. Osamu Inoue. *Nintendo Magic*. New York: Vertical, 2001. Print. 149.

2. Ibid. 169.

3. "Nintendo Invites People to Get Up and Get Playing at Wii Games." *Nintendo*. Nintendo of American. 30 Jun. 2010. Web. 28 Oct. 2010.

4. Tae K. Kim. "The Future of Nintendo is Now." *GamePro*. GamePro Media. 21 May 2010. Web. 28 Oct. 2010.

5. Osamu Inoue. *Nintendo Magic*. New York: Vertical, 2001. Print. 204.

6. Ibid. 169.

7. David Sheff. *Game Over: How Nintendo Zapped an American Industry, Captured Your Dollars, and Enslaved Your Children*. New York: Random, 1993. Print. 10.

8. "Shigeru Miyamoto Interviews." *Miyamoto Shrine*. n.p. 17 Mar. 2003. Web. 28 Oct. 2010.

INDEX

ABOUT THE AUTHOR

Mary Firestone has written more than 30 books for young readers. Her work has also appeared in a variety of Minnesota magazines and newspapers. She was a finalist in the Midwest Book Awards for her book *Dayton's Department.* She lives in St. Paul, Minnesota.

PHOTO CREDITS